DANDY BOGAN

Dandy Bogan

∽ SELECTED POEMS

Nick Ascroft

BOATWHISTLE BOOKS

First published in 2018
by Boatwhistle Books
22 Gloucester Road
Twickenham
London TW2 6NE
United Kingdom

www.boatwhistle.com

© Nick Ascroft 2018

Typeset in Minion by Boatwhistle

A catalogue record for this book
is available from the British Library

ISBN 978-1-911052-03-6

Printed in the United Kingdom by TJ International, Padstow,
on 80 gsm Munken Premium paper

Contents

◦ PART I
Elephantiasis of the Bollock (NEW POEMS)

Self-Planting of Evidence 3
Your Mother 4
Art Is Weak 6
Slung Across the Cat 8
Spring Is Sick with Child 10
Mixed Indoor Soccer Oaf 12
The Brain 13
Phrase Hack 14

◦ PART II
from *Back with the Human Condition* (2016)

Euphoria 19
Dumplings 20
Sad Goose 22
The For 23
But For 25
The Osney Hag 26
Shortcuts to the Art 28
House, Kid, Dog 30
House, Kid, Dog 32
The Lord of Work 34
So Angry 36

༄ PART III
from *Nonsense* (2003)

Ignis Fatuus 41
The Polar Birds 43
The 27th of December: at: 44
The Deathbeds of the Hospital 45
Misprescription 46
In a Locker, Desire 48
Chimps Can't Dance 50
Chimps Don't Laugh 51
Storm 52
Doesn't Have a Name 53
Waiter! 54

༄ PART IV
from *From the Author Of* (2000)

My Favourite 59
It's a Sad Place, the Country 62
Steven's Heavy Hammer 63
The Horse by the Seaside 64
Method Actor Hairy 66
The Holly and the Ivy 67

ᙯ PART V
Unpublishable (OLDER POEMS)

How Birds Lost Their Fingers 71
Hugh and the Humanish Condition 72
Mm, Yeah, Absolutely 74
Cockfight 75
Edgar the Godwit 76
The Crawly-Creep 78
Justice Fucus 79
An Arch Back-Bender, Nous and Some
    Polioed Portfolio 80
The Back of Me 83
The Anatomy of the Stars 84
Night 85

Acknowledgements 87

Part I

Elephantiasis of the Bollock

 NEW POEMS

Self-Planting of Evidence

I vacillate between the expedient and the
fastidious: write it on the corner of a nearby receipt
or go and fetch a clean piece of paper and welcome
the ease of the experience.
I use a pentacle instead of an asterisk

when I make bullet lists in pen.
I appreciate the madness of living and its balance of
    wild risks,
but without their wildness and imaginable danger
    the thing
would be worse.
True I suspect for lions and cheetahs, our old cousins and

acquaintances of the savannah. Things to avoid meet
emotions of deterrent
and attractors thrill, the self-abuse of decision-making.
Their fear of missing the mark on the
back of the hartebeest's leg feels awful, and

the delight of the kill drags them around
like greyhounds. How does it feel? No
different to yourself, the wordless chemical torture
of the inner awareness.
It's only fear that makes me hide the truth.

Your Mother

I. PREEYA

I need to wear a Cinderella dress.
It's after school. We're on the special sofa
where we air and solve things, though for
this catastrophe, I have to press
the point: I *need* to go to costume day
tomorrow in the dress. My monologue
gets tearful: I will never wear that frog
disguise again! Mum listens, says OK.
We beeline for the car, me at her hem,
and make it to the shop before it shuts.
She buys the fabric, draws a pattern, cuts
it out and has it sewn by 5 a.m.
I wake to find my golden perfect raiment,
my friends who gag in jealousy, her payment.

II. ALL THE MARCHES

The autumns that incinerated by,
the 1980s' dusk ablaze with pinks
and cherries in a phased Dunedin sky
or Adelaide's, the autumns as she slinks
around the lounge, her swaying perm so tall,
and Whitney Houston gurgles from the hall.
Ayutthaya's hot seasons and the Wirral's
spring all burn with rain. We pass the murals
in the Metro – Michigan! The squirrels! –
and fight to numb a thought whose epidurals
find us in Morocco, just a hose
to wash with, though the Berbers smell of rose.
There's part of us still at the garden mall
with Whitney Houston playing to the sprawl.

Art Is Weak

Conceptual art is not so empty sleeved
and brained. I think of Ai Weiwei's exhibit
spread across the Turbine Hall. Conceived
as interactive, we had to ad lib it
when, declared a health and safety hazard,
they cordoned off the artwork's sea of porcelain
seeds, and threat of noxious dust motes, as would
any fear us Mongols and our horsemen.
Instead of wading through the work, the rub
of seeds against the shins – *each little member,
each among the hordes, another schlub* –
I thought, detached, of that inert September,
of Nisha Pillai in the early hours
ad libbing over footage of the towers.

The planes impacting into steel sear
their image to the dark's imagination.
Conceptual art cannot at all compare
to it, so deft and cold in orchestration.
To dream it up, its vivid manifesto:
the first plane brought the news crews to the market,
the second a magician's flash, and presto
quiet to ourselves we said, 'Good target.'

The corporate heart of wealth, the miracle
America erected, bubble-wrapped
in brutalism: no empirical
mindset denies that 'blameless' is inapt.
But whispered, lest our ears misunderstand
and think we deem bin Laden's sculpture grand.

Conceptual art is tainted by the sheik's
set piece. And architecture too. The deed will
live in folklore longer than the blunt mistakes
that followed in response. It's his cathedral,
half-made like Gaudí's vast basilica
of holy folly, as indelibly
affecting, primary with blood's acrylic. The
escaping suicides from zealotry
and fire rained like fish, and Nisha Pillai
tried to summarise. I watched, was high,
and noodled with my pen, considered: 'Will I?
Sum up an act that suffers no reply?
In verse?' I could've. Poems are benign,
till Erdoğan kills thousands with a line.

Slung Across the Cat

In the evenings, slung across the cat,
we watched TV.
It wasn't some rattling sound in the corner that we talked
    over,
passed into the room and out of,
stood in front of with our arses towards it
and our rabbit teeth caught in a sneer,
or drifted away from and forgot about.
We positioned ourselves across from the great wide screen
and studied it.
There were many species of things we sought out
in our channel-flipping
and booking-in.

Tension was an essential:
mortal tension, anxiety,
shrieked tension, sublimated tension,
irony.
It was the taboo we were seeking out.
It was irreverence,
culture-secret Tourette's.
We wanted the television to sting us with shock.
And what we saw in psychopathy and horror was a
    reminder of
our thinness and fragility,
a shin-splinting for the sedentary mind.
We remarked in the silences.

You favoured dialogue and its idealised theatre of
human utterance.
You favoured the swordplay of words,
artful circumlocutions divorced from the stagnating
   circles
real human interaction stuttered in
like scumborne fly-legs.
I favoured the ease and economy of stylists and editors.
My eyes grazed light-handed production design,
the deft costumiery and lighting, eating it
with a sloth's fingers.
We admired storytelling,
the tale well told,

the playing off of genre,
and the well-rubbed routes of narrative headway,
the counterpoint,
the beauty of slick foreshadowing,
and the beauty of blunt foreshadowing.
We were moved by performance,
the fiction inhabited.
We were moved by the suffering,
the howling and tears and fury
or the stoical bearing of it.
The cat liked stillness and soporific mid-tones.
It affected tolerance.

Spring Is Sick with Child

Grey and morning-sick, spring
nurses itself like a pelican,
skimming a spoonbill of Cook Strait
ice water, and vomiting it back
onto Wellington in a trimester of rain.
The other seasons look on and quack
inanities. Summer coos from afar.
Summer blurts. Summer says of spring's

grey lump, you must be so happy.
Winter is unfiltered. Winter doesn't
want to dance on sugar-coated
eggshells. It wishes spring
to entertain no false hope: this
will get worse. Autumn mansplains
through its duck beard that spring
shouldn't be eating the Camembert.

Put it down it says, as heads turn.
Put it down, the only thing that
is bringing any comfort. The weeks
puke on. Spring's bud swells
inside it like a rolling wave of corn
and petals. It rains apple juice. It
rains pasta sauce. It rains yoghurt
and olive oil. The barometer stinks,

lurching in the wind, towards its eyrie,
a thrush's nest in a gutter's attic,
curry hot, freezer cold. Just colossally,
diarhhoeally dreck: the outside is
the open souvlaki of a nappy in wait.
On the tin roof, a kaka retches
and tweets the season's headache.
Ice water. Grey, regurgitated rain.

Mixed Indoor Soccer Oaf

Amid the hurly burly I can barely
form a memory, my mind a deluge
of mechanics. I allow the Quaaludes
of some inner animal to smear the
intellectual access to my motor
choices. I become subliminal.
Some gallants back off so that women will
have time to play the ball; I give no quarter.
I'm gender blind, though larger – less dilute –
than once I was. I tread on one's toe, slip
past her, then slam the next one with a hip.
They're skittled, wounded on the ground. I shoot
and score. The brunette seethes reproach, the blonde just
holds her foot. I blame the vast unconscious.

The Brain

You can't just be built to tolerance. There has to be a buffer in case of more extreme phenomena. The organ of the skull is no different from the one that pumps all the blood cells about. Could the aorta handle triple the work in a time of exceptional demand? Naturally. So to reveal the concealed depths of the brain's abilities, one must put it under stress.

Ionised gases emit light of varying colours.

Phrase Hack

As dry as ice.
    As wet as a whistle.
        As clean as a clergyman's clavicle.

Grayden depressed the receive-call button on his headpiece and yawned
his automated greeting:
'Welcome, hello, and can I or (why would I or) how can I help you?'

As Greek as to me all.
    As twice as the knock of how often the postman.
        As hotly as from off its tin roof the cat as
            anticipated.

Just as gain does, no gain involves a concomitant dollop of agony. No gain, pain.
If he wasn't the kind of depressing in a cheerleading outfit one offers
awareness-raising to he would tell it with pom-poms: pee aggressive, P-E
    E-E-E
        E-E-E-E
            aggressive.

As cold as a baby's coffin.
   As soft as a cell.
      As clear as a jelly.

Grayden's mother, also called Grayden, worked at the bureau of
schadenfreude, sturm und angst, or births, deaths and marriages.
'It's me,' she retorted, hanging up on him.

As wide as a nun's garden.
   As shaggy as a story of a dog in the 1970s.
      As sweet as silk.

Part II

from *Back with the Human Condition*

 2016

Euphoria

Happiness is diaphanous,
sylphish, ephemeral, all of the *ph* words, i.e.
Greek, i.e. whose nature, whose physique is

pure,
mythic, appreciable only
to the lonely older senses:

the pure ruins in the winter of their summer.

We are subject to it, like the cold –
whose phrases are as prime, as old and bare.
Fuck it's cold. I love your hair.

Dumplings

Throw him out like dough on a flour-dusted table,

put your wrists into it, your back – hh   sacrum, hips,
get a knee up, weight your thick of your femur from
up your upper leg to its lock: let him, in your knuckles

and short breaths, feel – ff – hh – ff – it, the dumpling
furl of your pelvic girdle. Left to moisten, commingle,
they've been aching thirty minutes

under a sultry towel, while you slit and drained
the bok choy (*paâk ts'òi*: white vegetable – ff – hh –
gamine little vegetable) and indexed it in ground pork,

just a zaftig waft of scent to salve: dry sherry and
ginger, sweat-odouring scallions, and its oil's bitter
    sesame.
Throw him out like the dough of a dumpling skin,

ease him onto his chest on a dusted table.
And engrossed in it, licking like a gecko, roll him.
The dowel works the handfuls of dough to skins

of a half-moon, and furrows pleats of their outer arc.
Everything has waited to steam in clammy bamboo: the
soyabeans and wheat fermenting the salted months

to sauce; him, salty lipped, eyes like cold water and flour,
and a suppler dough in the lower boil;
and you – ff – parched – hh – ff – hand-feeding,

arched – hh – one knee up on a kitchen chair.

Sad Goose

                    The
                  subdued
                  hues, on
                    the
                    nape
                    of a
goose, of night, as it lands,
loose in its story, creaking to the words
of the wind the shuddering of memory,
bend into the grey of white. A triangle of
awny goose tongue licks at its umami
feathers. The comfort of fat, it says
of itself, in the jars I keep lost

at the back of the high hoard of shelves I close my eyes and wander among. It cradles its wings in its collar, stretches, looking now with a beak pursed to an O, long as the note unsung and balanced taper-like on an egg of goose body – the furious elation of stars above.

The For

for Michelle and Simon

For richer and better, for, by scatty luck, please,
an unechoey phoneline when one's overseas.

For passion, precision, for by planning ahead
Friday's wrapped up, Monday not yet in bed.

From Delhi to Chile, from New York and glory
to the dog-on-wood tick from a floor in Karori.

For art and refinement, for TV and beer,
a considerate tongue and a tolerant ear.

For the world and inhabitants; nature and science.
For a trouble-free car and the latest appliance.

In diplomacy tranquil, in bargaining zealous,
for a cut-price that leaves friends and family jealous.

For kitchenware, creams, haberdashery, socks,
for bathware and hardware, spatulas, woks.

For a love that ensures not to worry or fret
but burns in the mouth like a curry does (*phet*).

For a terrible film, but one sobs like a goose,
and one would object, but well, what's the use.

For smells and for screeches, for measles and mumps,
for after-work tetchy and premenstrual grumps.

For richer, for better, till death has them dead
(their thoughts idling fogwise from lounge-room to bed).

For wife and her husband – and inside her the ween –
to sit sweet in their family like snug mangosteen.

But For

I lowered myself
like a bear's arm into another wineglass.
Reconstruct how you think of me. I'm tall
but small-shouldered. Womanly of hip.
Little perturbations of a puddle upset me.

Rain streaks a grey air like thought.
Bending, I nudge the glass with my face.
Don't rear back mantis-like, I say to it in a hush, the
    outside is
bearable and undreary.
My ears are distracted from the hissing by first a goose

somewhere in the overhead near-dark creaking like a
    door, then
a computer. In the best of the transitive outside
I would describe there repetitively but for being seen
    and mulled
winelike upon the apices and worsts or otherwise put the
    shudderings
of the inner palate but for the air wobbling not

at our say so on the auditory nerves
in this goosecreak and blotted-out jingle of its evening.
Sleepy, I am unverbose but mistaken, the
shaky finger of a gist I inherited
with the patter.

The Osney Hag

I.

No code is uttered from the shopfloor tannoy.

My manager, Muruj, just mutters, 'Anne,
oi get yourself to undergarments, look,'
and points a pen along her aproned dress:
the Osney Hag has entered M&S,
bedecked in bags that hang from every hook –
her fingers, teeth and in each elbow's crook –
and bags within, like onions lathering
her coiled mind. I sweep the gathering
detritus bobbing in her wake. We brook
no trespass (ugh, one bag has our logo).
I make it felt: the foodhall is a no go.
Her figure shrinks away, doglike and motley,

and lumbers bag-encumbered on to Botley.

II.

The Osney Hag returns to me in dreams.

Her volatile eye in close-up – glimpse-
surmising my role supervising – seems
a melancholy moon, but its eclipse
that starts in bag-clenched spasms of her lips,
if not a smile, is a memory
of one. She feints with outstretched fingertips
to brush her touch of careworn emery
against a rack of bras, then darts to starboard,
and, perceiving that I've followed, lists
abruptly off to port. I never harboured
notions I was high or grand, but twists
of fortune find me plodding to a beat

whose half-shod feet my dreams and I repeat.

Shortcuts to the Art

Half of the light, the soft light, the light made into a coat
>hanger,
or an exact tractor over the armchair.
The light made a series of open-ended questions
on a forearm, the soft churn and chuck
of the desklamp.

What is it about lightly, the lightliness, the grunt volume of
limpness and luminance, the flux of lux, what's so
>salubrious in it?
What is your bung vision of the tradition? A series of polite
obsessions.
It's this:
>I have made light into toner.
>It's a grit that
>>sclurges into the
>wringer, glints like
>>grain-sand into the
>>pages into print.

What is it about slowly? What slows, what so whets and
>slows our
wits
as slo-mo?

    It's the tilt

    on the head

       of a film
the dog's watching.
The buzz, the razz, the tizz over the split-seconds low-lit,
the extra sexual split-sections in the slo-mo. Itty. Precious.
The bonus footage per yardage of cinematography.
The light, the light, the slow.

House, Kid, Dog

House, kid, dog: file under things to regret as the years avalanche in.
Birthdays are miserable, let's not pretend otherwise.
Like Christmas, weeping alone on the toilet.
I was convinced insurance was a racket, then the earthquake.
When you were ill and needed me, I was on holiday, bored.

Were cities ever compassionate, or always these shuffling scarecrows?
The rich get nouveau richer.
The poor get richer too, but everything costs more.
We get richer but bitterer.
We get sicker, weaker, blander but less patient with each other.

Where's the fire of youth?
Where's the pessimism of youth that felt cool and not yet terrifying?
I prefer your birthday to mine, out of spite.
Nostalgia's like a meal of sand.
We have no regrets because we didn't do anything.

Our successes were years ago and now small, but we
    cling on with our teeth.
Everybody is younger and more celebrated than us.
Our families find us selfish.
Our neighbours hate us.
We still torture ourselves with dreams.

The grass will be greener under a mountain of debt.
The grass will be greener when our child abandons us.
The grass will be greener when the dog shits on it.
There was always a certain shame in pride.
But the truth is uglier: all pride is shame.

House, Kid, Dog

House, kid, dog: we sink our teeth into the gristle of living.
Birthdays are suffered with grace: we die celebrating.
Like Christmas, gagging on gooseflesh.
It's humbling and wonderful, to be returned to nothing.
In your despair, I emailed hugs.

History is written by the writers of history.
The rich get funnier.
The poor get smallpox, and we laugh at them.
We get richer but persevere.
We get fatter and greyer, and laser eye surgery.

Young people are awful.
They want to change the world, so let them try and fail.
I prefer your birthday to mine, out of sweetness and
    sycophancy.
No, pleasure is timeless, guiltless.
And regrets are for the half-hearted, and John Dolan.

Our anxieties are vainglorious, if elegant in their spidersilk
    of misery.
The discerning few respect us.
Our families can't find us.
The neighbours are hidden behind their hedges.
They leave us to the sins of aspiration.

Our house will be a summoning of wood and light.
Our child will be short and strange.
We'll never get a fucking dog.
Living is a pratfall but clock me around the head with it.
Stand proud: small, powerful, appalling.

The Lord of Work

I worked through lunch.
I worked through dinner, through the night and through
    breakfast.
I worked through an otherwise relaxing shower.

I worked through weekends and public holidays.
I worked on the Sabbath. I worked through Ramadan.
I worked through Kwanzaa.

I worked through 'Welcome to the Working Week' by
    Elvis Costello.
I worked through the Lou Reed song 'Don't Talk to Me
    about Work'.
I worked through 'This Woman's Work' by Kate Bush.

I paused only to make like I thought I was going to
    sneeze.
Then worked through the sneeze itself when it came.
I worked through the hiccups, the chicken pox and the
    manflu.

I worked through Tropical Cyclone Pam.
I worked through the Iranian nuclear deal.
I worked through the Tour de France.

I worked with my eyes closed.
I worked hands-free.
I worked with ergonomic equipment and still developed epicondylitis.

I worked while I slept, like the Buddha.
I worked while I was not working, like the Zen Buddha.
I worked as I lay reading *As I Lay Dying* by William Faulkner.

I worked as I lay dying.
You can't work when you're dead.
But I'll work when I'm dead like Jesus, or Sisyphus.

So Angry

for Kate on the occasion of her 31st birthday

Hark. Harken.
The morning sky is peridot dark.
As the hours crunch, it will only darken.
Hark, harken. The fark? The alarm.
The kraken.

You writhe a tentacle from the sea of bed, it slaps at
    glasses, shoes,
an unread tome – ah, the phone – and taps the snooze.
We float out into the city wasteland like litter.
Flitting over fox turds, and stuttering lamplight and Polish
and the ghost of last night's killer, whispering bismillah.

As beautiful as an icicle and as frozen
in the blanketless air, your thoughts go jangly.
You are so angry.
The amber light on the Oyster reader is tutted awake,
    as your card asks it
to calculate the girth of its net worth.

We beep like sheep
our routines of digital confetti.
The Tube poles are sweaty.
The eyes are hot, who frot, they sneeze spaghetti
in a sauce of mange and HPV.

One lady has the breath of an anchovy.
As beautiful and sick as a sausage, you summon a lemon
    lozenge.
Aunty Britain. So cold, so thick with dark
and funk and sick.
Her ganglia grow angrier.

The dungeon of London.
So wilfully pants backward with its buck teeth stuck in its
    nineteenth century.
So catastrophically bollock-follicle choleric and diabolical.
(A land awaits of flax and light and breeze
and the dangling limbs of orange trees.)

Part III

from *Nonsense*

 2003

Ignis Fatuus

Back when before I saw that will-o'-the-wisp hovering
    over the crops
on the low paddock by the swamp, when before I even
    tried to run some sheep
on the low paddock for a few weeks and by the morning
    half of them'd be cast,
I've always known somehow that my dead daughter's
    soul was fenced in there,
clawing her way out of the bogs that sink into the pit of
    the swamp.

No, yeah it was on a spring night, and it'd been up last
    night and mawing at the night
like a phosphorescent fish and so I was down there in
    the dip where I ford
over the trench of the main bog and when it trotted its
    way up again I took its
picture on my old man's old camera. And I seen it there,
    in the detail of the central
floating lantern, definite palm and fingers of my dead
    little Veronica.

She's doing like I told when we're at the beach with the
    rip in. She's
keeping one arm up out of the water, so Daddy can see
    her. I'm always tending
that tobacco paddock. Sometimes in the middle of the
    night I have to get up, eh,
and steal over the back past the sleeping new cows, over
    the slaughterpit,
and down the slope through the blackberries to break
    my back

in that low paddock.

The Polar Birds

You know about Moses and the burning bush, Richard?
Uh, Moses was astounded by the clear voice in
the fire's noise. Is the sun, uh, God setting
underneath the purple
clouds where the sea's caught fire, Richard?

Look, um look now, a pantomime sea lion. And
the oystercatchers look like spears thrown by an,
uh, army of Israelites.
But in their little peeping

souls, they are good. They are good husbands
and wives of birds looking for some pudding
in the sand dunes. Oh they are shrill birds, Richard.
Uh, the noise really sticks
in the ears like the secret love poetry of nurses.

The 27th of December: at:

'The time the chemist's car got robbed, because
they still require medicine around
the tide of Christmas, Grandad would've drowned
if left alone in – like his neighbour was:

'That morning, officer, because you can't
be sure there'll always be a nurse to come
and dress and doctor him – *if there were some
good laws concerning deathbeds* – but there aren't:

'While half your pill run went unmedicated
I'd had to show a bit of bloody moxie.
With no professional, I'd stood in as proxy
nurse: *trial via fire educated*.'

The cop unclicked his pen, said bye, and thanks.
I sighed. My shoulder bag was packed with tranqs.

The Deathbeds of the Hospital

The creak of a hinge waits to creak,
under inoculating walls that wait,
above a metal bed that waits to creak
under the ever-lessening weight of our torso with limbs,
limbs that wait to slack, crossed on our torso
like wreaths.

There's a chart that waits to warm under a photocopier,
to warm under the scrutiny of a nurse's hands
and the pen-hand of an arm in a shroud of a sleeve.

A draught from a ward door edges a daily round
to the ankle height above a square of bare carpet,
where the ankles of a man at a bedside
will inevitably give. And our face congested in a pillow
will inevitably congest, and give.

A compulsory sheet struggles in the wash.
A vacated room is filled and will vacate,
and a song on a bar stereo wobbles and
we sing along in our head, rolling a tune
like the rolling circles of our arteries, compulsory veins.

Misprescription

During the winter curfews the household of Mr
and Mrs Horizontal would get into the airing cupboard
and warm their circulations on the dog.
All they had to eat were acorns and baking soda.
They were both miserably sad and both of them

had tuberculosis. One bitterly cold evening
after their children had died of frostbite,
and Mr Horizontal had caught his fingers in the car
door, an incredibly fortunate and uplifting set
of circumstances ploughed their way like a ray of light

into the once dingy and sealed-off refrigerator

of their lives. The war ended, the winter subsided,

they fell in love, the dog nabbed second place

in a vivisection pageant and through it all
Myrtle Horizontal's face slowly peeled out
of the swamped gloom that had held it
downcast and drab for so many years of footcramp and
water-up-the-nose, allergies, side effects, and

masterly catastrophes of misprescription leading
to blindness. A smile formed in time lapse photography
on her face, like maggots devouring a sparrow,
and she knew she was faking it, laundering it out –
she felt awful, *awful*, and worse for feeling it.

In a Locker, Desire

I keep a caricature of myself in every airport,
to slip into like a pool of cement.

It's easy to forget
which perfunctory performance,
which hobgoblin of manners,
which desolate expression to approach
the lost luggage and baggage clerk with,
where on the forehead to fawn
the back of my hand.

I've got a hundred forged passports with
the same perfected expression
stencilled into the photograph, pensive.
I've always had it
that a shrewd face beats a shrewd brain.
I've always had it
that a well-practised outlook beats a better one.

And if I've always had it,
then I'll wake up with it tomorrow
like a rash.
In the inconsistencies of countries,
the integrity of my indignity
is like a locker in every airport.
There's a chain of keys I keep in

a thousand identical shoulder bags,
and leave behind in
a thousand identical picture theatres.
It's easy to forget where best to forget a thing.
But the drop and exchange for my contact,
and I do my own, has a thousand identical
backup plans.

If I'm lost then,
I'm lost in a locker lounge
at every airport, so I'm found again,
hamming at a counter. And I'll lope aboard
the unadjusted flight schedule,
before the delay –
that unaccountable minute

emanating from where my lost key chain left it,
ticking, a horrible thistle of wires,

in a locker, desire.

Chimps Can't Dance

I posit a civilisation that dawdled
through numbing millennia, clinging
desperately to the darkest of ages, filling their
encyclopaedic heads with as much mumbo-jumbo,
as many rites and dance steps as could get them
into bed. You only have to sift through the genetic

baggage bequeathed us
to despair. *Honestly*, I mean *really*.
This repertoire of spasms and contortions,
how it ever outbred the hairier, more demure
assignations, issuing from more prognathic
jaws and svelte heads, I'll never comprehend.

Chimps Don't Laugh

Junk all words.
Probe only into a block of residents by the way they laugh:
Who was a laugh addressed to?
Who laughs first? And follows?
Who loudest clapping their calves? Who last?

Like English is German by
a line, a people of speakers
bent, contorted, polluted over time,
laughter is chimpanzee.
See our small bands and families
of panting australopithecines,

conveying in the hooting flats
of autistic society – laughing our
subjugations,
under the noise of words.
Junk all words; instinct-think in the unthinkable language

of screaming and laughter.

Storm

The storm has passed, that came before the calm.
Another year has combed its beard since, since
the calm, and all the moments suffered, all the harm,
is past, the storm that razed now let to rinse

the drains. He heard it shatter from the trunk,
outside at 3 a.m., an upper section
decades old. A single witness drunk
on rain and vodka wept his introspection

while I slept above in rattled fits.
It broke a word, the limb that was a tree
itself, prostrated on our path, and its
now amputated other half above, to be

alive, and calm. (The calm – like when you died.)
The tree remained; the tree was moved aside.

Doesn't Have a Name

My attic isn't an attic.
There are no attics.
The marsupial in my attic isn't a marsupial
because it doesn't have a name.
The circuit on the heater clicking, isn't clicking.
There's no clicking. What's a click?
Nothing makes a click.
And nothing is cold. It's not colder
in the bathroom. Nothing is a bathroom.
And when I wake up
and see a face, I don't.
I don't wake up. Nothing wakes
and sees faces. There is no face because it
doesn't have a name, and there's no I wake,
no I see, because it
doesn't have a name.

Waiter!

Your clavicles are as lovely as hedgehogs.
Clang, slung under two cavities in your cranium,
    ding-a-ling-a-ling,
your ears are as tiny as two little brass clochette bells.
And Allah. A good cut beaucoup longer than
the fattest word in the dictionary are your wrists.
If you were a cabbage, I'd let you stay in a windowbox
outside my spare room.

There's the sun through the monsoon,
barely brighter than a break-light,
sack-racing itself nowhere over the skyline.
Cameriere! The introuvable bubble of the atmosphere!
Let the sky fill with bats and planes,
let all the xenon get fluffed up by albatrosses and rain, and
slip your jambled head on the ironboard of my lap,
    my leeble,
my queeble, my quiebchen.

I am a doctor's library, a dishwasher
froth of red pipes and unwiped hands. And your dining
    room, slam,
whoops, that's a tray spilt, the pressurestorm gets
under the draughts, and shrinks hallways,
confuses the hinges of doors – your fine dining room
is a passport to a password to a buspass. Plant your
    pamplemousse

on the sideboard, and brood it all to pieces.
Your knee joints are clickier than firemen,
your reach could stretch behind the luxuriest of fridges,
and the chew on you, the way you hold a hairbrush,
the *the* of the articality of you.
If it was a smell it'd be wet rocks and old clocks. And I'd
    be a shy
breather in, another sojourner with a secret sniff.

Part IV

from *From the Author Of*

 2000

My Favourite

YEARS OF PRACTISING PREFERRING
HER VEGETABLES TO DESSERT

My favourite reminds me of a man I knew
called Albert.
His skin was the kind of black
you could fall into.
I saw him lift a house with one hand and
I believe if he trod too heavily
on the earth
someone would die in Spain.
My favourite differs.

It is her social grace that can kill Spaniards,
her lungs that lift houses and
the blackness of her conversation that
I could fall into.

I once slept with the entire population
of Dunedin, obviously
I in my bed they in theirs, but
the following morning
we all were gripped by a state of uneasiness,
of humming, whistling and hedging,
an awkward silence
broken only by the loud smiling of my favourite
for unease is her fruit and sustenance.

But
don't mistake me.

As my favourite and I walk in opposite directions,
I pray the world truly is round,

that we may crack our skulls together once more.

DELICATELY, YET BLEEDING, IN HER PASSENGER SEAT

I gathered my favourite was either
a drop too much Mongoloid or
a Turkish articulatory delight but
there we were
three thousand years ago
slung across the same horse in Asia Minor or
beneath the Urals –
I forget now.
I can't remember what the argument was over but

when it was over I left the east and
went west and north.
I went south.
Now reunited

we drive in opposite directions.
But
don't mistake me.
I pray that Galileo's calculations were sound,
that I may shatter my windscreen,
flip my ankles over my head and
my arse over my ankles
to shatter my favourite's windscreen and
land delicately, yet bleeding,

in her passenger seat.

It's a Sad Place, the Country

The eldest son riding on the back
of his father's ute says to himself, that magpie
will guard my soul.
It's a sad place, the country. Earlier
this morning his father had a word with
the bathroom mirror, here we go.

The burden of the farm will rest
on this child's little shoulders one day
but his thoughts are somewhere else.
He'd like to hug himself around one of those sheep,
squeeze it like a beach ball.

The three of them are headed out
to a paddock somewhere, where willows bank
a dry creek, resigned.
His younger brother yells over the noise,
in a fight, who would win over who,
a toi-toi or a flax bush.

Steven's Heavy Hammer

Confound Steven into the floorboards, and beneath to hell

and my hell, the hell of a head and its queen's eggs housed
in a precarious shell of skull.

No officer or money-mad advocate would dare harm a hair
on his child's head, nor wiggy judiciary bolt him into the
    prison
his dolt head deserves and worse.
To the corner of the kindergarten grant him a savancy
to his idiot. Have it blow on him like a hammer from his
bully hands. Torment back the hormones

of the torment at his rougher hands that my bones and
delicate honed brain must suffer at.

The Horse by the Seaside

At the Friendly Bay fair they used to sell
rides on a horse with no legs

It'd taught itself to wriggle
its shoulders, its throat and haunches
so that it squirmed along like a caterpillar.
As their children buck in terror on its back
anxious parents covered their delight
with their hands.
Before it was shot, groups of girls
and boys used to come in the evenings, call it names
and pelt it with stones and cans.

It would neigh soft throaty complaints,
more like the bleating of a sheep or
a weak cricket.
I don't remember when it had to be withdrawn
from service. The first Sunday I noticed
it not there, however, I remember that:
I secured first prize in a beauty pageant;
I was only six. It was a fat thin-eyed boy
that the judges had overlooked who broke its back.

As its mane flared up it must've burst
into tears, relief, agony. It was a dumb beast.
It should've dreamt of a church by the seaside,
of a woman in the aisle, leaving the lectern.
It should've seen her face, held still
like the statue of a saint,
and there, as she felt herself grinding
through motions of the legs and arms, slight
twists of the hip, uncharacteristic of a statue,

then her face would break, like an egg,
like a lightbulb, like an aquarium.

Method Actor Hairy

The orang-utan agonised out of his wrinkled slumber.

He dazily donned a shirt, a tie, put his feet on, abluted,
then freighted his fat arse on a train of sleepy apes
to the hovel of his office.

Jeez, the noise in that place, the hee-hawing of fanged
muzzles, the barked orders and wheezy cringing,
the pecking order gnashing and squeaking
from slovenly desktops, and hoo-hoo-hoo, jeez,
hooting in the rafters, some dim office gibbon, crazed,
abetting himself into a fury of pure majestical
    obsequium.
The orang-utan pinched the bridge of his nose.
He imagined the hours snaking away, pictured the
    weekend
rattling at their end and a bar
littered with method actor injuns, lying dead in piles.

He conjured the dry tenderfoot squeam boiling him
    awake
sometime on the baffled Sunday,
his hands smelling of rubber.

The Holly and the Ivy

They swing,
she with her head,
he with his hips,
in slow sexual revolutions.

He looks at her
like a mental hospital.
She touches his chest
like a stethoscope.

If love is a restaurant
they are seated by a window
looking down at
a thousand corpses

burying themselves,

thinking – that could be you,
that could be me.

Part V

Unpublishable

 OLDER POEMS

How Birds Lost Their Fingers

The sky is a void;
one can hold on to nothing
for only so long.

Hugh and the Humanish Condition

In the South Pacific nation
of the people-climbers,
sometimes suddenly out of some long grasses
would spring a small jockey-sized
man. He'd get up on your back
and no matter how you thrashed about,
how much you bit at him
and whinneyed for him to – sir, exit my back! –
he remained squinting back at you, up there,
twisting your ear with a fingernail impaled
underneath in a nerve.
The pinching-crab they called it.
I was there twenty years under the yoke of one of them.

I'd arrived at nineteen, left thirty years later,
a freed slave with a crooked back and soul.

It wasn't that I was that really
put upon or anything.
After a while we'd become – hum – chummy.
And it's not as though I didn't plot to unlock his
knee-grip in the night and slip off,
and I'd've would've loved to've done,
but they're a brilliantly civilised bunch
of precision machines,
the Austronesian people-climbers.
He'd always be in the habit of spotting

any plotting I might've been considering to conduct.
It was the gait of the pacing, and apparently
some indicative neck rash.
In the end they all give in and I did
just to shut him up, the buzziness,
the rasping eekiness, his nasally annoying voice.

And likewise at the end,
that was it again too, his horrible
tormenting seagull caterwaul, his bark – *Hark
Hugh, no, tarry or stray, yet findeth I thy replacement.
Hark, hark Hugh, Hugh hark.*
I was Hugh of the humiliations.
Ow, the scissors through that last little guilty gristle
of pride – my bony knees bonking together
down the gangplank, clank bang,
into Auckland airport,
obsolete.

Mm, Yeah, Absolutely

I was being preverbal
when I stumbled out of company
and had an autobiographical
moment in the bathroom.

It was slow-paced and sentimental.
It suffered puncture under its self-indulgence.
It was all right if I have to
suck up about it.

But achoo it happened. And doltish
and sheepish, it all got jotted out over the next
few months, while the sticky
nerdy knowitalls said

that it wasn't any good.

Cockfight

The swelter in the crowd
of glazed bare legs
crept around the bodies at knee height
in a fug of air.
The seventeen-year-old with the black one held his bird
by its legs
– thin and purpled like his –
its beak away from him.
The older man
with a wispy moustache swatted at the comb
of his pied prize fighter with a practised backhand;
it reared
and jabbed the warmth
of empty air ahead of it.
Then he signalled the fight on.

Edgar the Godwit

'It's always going to be polite to say
what you've repeatedly been diagnosed as', says Norman
    Hemmingsen
at the box-window of the hospital reception,
'by specialist physicians and psychiatrists.'
They say wait at the soft chairs.

At the soft chairs he says, 'Yes,
I'm a wizard at the computers, no not a wizard so much,
    witch, a witch,
a black voodoo witch-priest, my fingerbones
rattling in the keypad, shaking the guide-stone.
I memorise spells for hours in the seminary

'of the computers section at the bookshop.
Here look I have a coin you know, the coin
that all the beggars of the world

'sieve the streets for, that was cast
from the meteorite metals of the Gomorrah stone.'
They take the coin and edge towards a clipboard and
    a blue-coat.
'It's a polite, a matter, a matter of
being polite.' And he summoned the thoughts

of speech and voice classes. 'Edgar the godwit.
Edgar the godwit lived at the top of Belleknowes.
He would tuck himself into his jacket, stride the tree-
    bridged ridge and
soar down Stuart Street, over only an
occasional taxi and one lone nightlong walker.'

The Crawly-Creep

Inside the child's ears concealed deep
enough to dodge the gaze of adults who
might peek inside to rummage through the view
for dirt, there lived a hairy crawly-creep,

a spider whom the child rightly blamed
for all his inabilities to think
of what to say, because the mental ink
that wrote the words to voice, the words enframed

in nervous pulses all across the brain,
was spread there by the spider's silk behind;
it made the sense that spoke the child's mind.
In bed at night he'd mutter and complain

about the tickling of the crawly-creep
that never stopped or thought to let him sleep.

Justice Fucus

Remit, recuse, sequester, err, the morning performed
    its arc into its afternoon.
Which, unmootably, was worse, *lud*.
The appellants were repugnant, whose counsels
    counselled offal, and at
para [137], the Act drained, sweaty, dumbstruck,
    I dissented.

I dissented, primer-fay-she, eggs-high-prophesy, over
    the everything.
But at para [138] – like this damn jammed stapler –
    blockage.
I tried Latin cum New Latin, cum pig Latin.
I threw it into a macro – subsections bled into

subsections – I tried unadulterated HTML. I tried
    Samoan.
Nil. Nihil. Ixnay. Leai se mea.
Up the balusters and bannisters out of the Robing Room
    and into the Law Library
the precedents laboured in the dust.

An Arch Back-Bender, Nous and Some Polioed Portfolio

Legislated sneaky – savvy? – skinnied-down into her skivvy, she's a flik-
flakking ribbon of red tape, a logistics legitimising prize walkover,
and a wheeze eh Nigel, huh Nigel, eh Gwen.
All we gotta purloin here, by the curl of their groin-fur are their sirships'
crunched atoms of hirsute undermistandings, then suture, simmer
and serve. Serve them back and too right by the fat ipso factos
we've siphoned into our feedboxes. I've been pusillanimising

and hippocampus downsizing around this company since before we was
lorises and lemurs. I've bunged, hiffed, embezzled more
gung-ho rambo bimbos into profit nozzles and tutus, sold more
money in honeypots to hotshots and guru zulus
than a backbench press harasser could hedge
their face off edgeways. Yassir, I been a longtime faucet,
mocha-chocolate-frosting on stale buns, and I done see know

my sticky business statistics, eh Nigel, hey Nigel, huh Gwen.
Take this bundle of raked twigs
tumbling up a run of slackjaw leers, while some backdoor

handshakes slam briefcases with pleased faces.
She's a militant refrigerant concocted to keep the big cogs
    incognisant.
To slip from fish to lizard, you gotta first fleece or grease
some dubious amphibious flippers, whippersnappers.

And this wicker bulimic is just the licky ticket in our steamy
sandy salamandery. Handstanding,
she's a salivator's sandwich which we dangle on a cord,

grandstanding, squat-eyed and bald-fangled. Whosemejib,
    consarn-cussing-
rhubarb-ahem-ahurrumphamejib. When I brown in the
    spring,
botulisment, and defer you – parlez vous? –
let you go off, reduce you – compringo? – then I'm back lost
in the Serengeti machete-work of it. Lingo limbo lost, bush-
    bashing brash
in the branches, just a cash-cow carnivore gnashing out the
    accounts
in his own fiscal cosmos. Y'all've all been felicitously illicitly

complicit in it. I'm a solid wallet of salt with shares
  in tears,
and shucks. Surely shucks. If I'm blubbing freebies
  I better sell a bit of
viscid advice. Underwrite your rented ears
where the pay-cheque's necking: heck there's a
gleaming leotard of a line, baranied in the beamwork just
waiting there sly to oblige. Through the ethicists and
  deficits,
plum-thumb the precipice, hey Gwendolyn – Nigel? –
  eh Nige.

The Back of Me

Anyone interested in my good side
will be glad to see the back of me.
As I check the horizon and
beneath
try to stop my farewell parties
being too gay.

I will marry my shoes and
honeymoon well away from
my well-wishers and couldn't-make-its and
especially those who for so long and
with such vigour
have desired my honeymoon.

The Anatomy of the Stars

I've got a bone to pick with you, old boy.
I've seen a world where any Lisa, any Tina,
any young honest Benjamin can rattle
their bike down any driveway, catch
a glimpse of any favourite star overhead
and their front teeth on a low branch.

I've seen people dream the dreams of
the unconscious, dreams you can hear,
coughing into the air conditioning,
dreams that if you stood in, you'd wipe
your shoe with your sleeve and burn your shirt.
Sit down, save your old bones, we have all night.

What have you been stirring in the stars?
What contortions of the constellations,
what paroxysms in the seas of space
have you been wreaking? I know you're there,
spread behind the clouds old thing, quieter
than a deaf man's brain, silently plotting.

Night

There's a jam bun of a bumblebee
that sings with its sting as it tears it into a mandolin:
unsex the nexus of the night.

*I'm the thorn in a thistle patch, an itch
on a notch of a knee,
annexing the light:*

unsex the nexus of the night.
And the doleful proletarian cells and the drones
that flex to drecks of self-insecticide

unsex the nexus of the night.

Acknowledgements

Massive thanks go to Victoria University Press, who published the three collections this book is mostly compiled from: *From the Author Of*, *Nonsense* and *Back with the Human Condition*.

Of the previously uncollected poems thanks go to the journals and anthologies that first published 'Art Is Weak' (*Landfall*), 'Mixed Indoor Soccer Oaf' (*Boots*), 'Justice Fucus' (*Blackmail Press*), 'Spring Is Sick with Child' (*Queen Mob's Tea House*), 'Phrase Hack' (*Turbine*), 'An Arch Backbender, Nous and Some Polioed Portfolio' (*Glottis*), 'The Anatomy of the Stars' (*Landfall*), 'The Back of Me' (*Sport*) and 'Night' (*Ika*).

Special thanks to Hamish Ironside of Boatwhistle for making this selection and his tireless attention to dovetail.

The book is dedicated to the house (Chez Cheez), the kid (Ames Perry Ascroft) and the cat (Kašpar).